LIFE

MISFIT

HIS LIFE

A POEM

GEORGE
BOWERING

ECW PRESS

Copyright © ECW PRESS, 2000

All rights reserved. No part of this publication may be reproduced, stored in a retrieval system, or transmitted in any form by any process — electronic, mechanical, photocopying, recording, or otherwise — without the prior written permission of ECW PRESS.

CANADIAN CATALOGUING IN PUBLICATION DATA

Bowering, George, 1935–
His life : a poem

ISBN 1-55022-408-5

1. Bowering, George, 1935– Poetry. I. Title.

PS8503.O875H57 2000   C811'.54   C00-930440-1
PR9199.3.B63H57 2000

A misFit book edited by Michael Holmes
Cover and text design by Tania Craan
Cover photo by Thies Bogner
Layout by Mary Bowness
Printed by Marc Veilleux

Distributed in Canada by General Distribution Services,
325 Humber Blvd., Toronto, Ontario M9W 7C3

Published by ECW PRESS
2120 Queen Street East, Suite 200,
Toronto, Ontario, M4E 1E2
www.ecw.ca/press

The publication of *His Life* has been generously supported by The Canada Council, the Ontario Arts Council, and the Government of Canada through the Book Publishing Industry Development Program. Canadá

Acknowledgements:

Twenty-three parts of this poem were published in 1991 as *Quarters*, a chapbook by Barry McKinnon at the Gorse Press. It won the bpNichol chapbook prize that year.

Other parts have been published in *West Coast Line*, *The Free Verse Anthology*, *Canadian Literature*, *The Capilano Review*, *Tads*, *Proserpine Press*, *Queen Street Quarterly*, and *House Organ*.

The versions here are somewhat changed.

for Angela & Thea.

SUMMER 1958. MERRITT

Days below the forest are becoming
hot, hot, hot, tritely
hot. Childhood days, when eating too much
is horrific.

Exploded words, like trees in a fire
cresting. Similes scarring a book,
not a sail in sight.

A letter from J. He wonders whether she
thinks of him. She didnt even sculpt him.
She can do whatever she wants to him.
He wonders if he'll see her again.

His grades have been mailed. He's doubly
anxious to see them. His, too. He wonders if
his father outdid him again.
        Classical
relation makes a family of us all.

FALL 1958. Vancouver

First day of lectures
in his third year of study

and Malcolm was alive,
Lowry, city full of parks.

It could have been his sixth year
but he regrets nothing, life

goes like episodes, Yankees win
again, dogs bark from wet yards.

They live on 20th near Oak Street,
where Jews go to the meat store,

the best writer in town is still
alive, mountains and their scant trees

far away. No one
is swinging a bat, the wet fields

have soccer posts, painted white
every year. The old loves, habitual

friendships, old memories re-enclose,
re-awake. But those books, ah

God.

WINTER 1958. Oliver

A legend
beginning to fade,
a noisy family
in a town without snow.

He cant flick his ashes in the fireplace.
It is a new electric heater.
You have entered the hill-straits —
a sea treads upon the hill-slopes.
There is nothing exactly
to do all day.
And yesterday went with the ice.

SPRING 1959. Vancouver

The National Hockey League with its
normality ends its season tomorrow, maybe
the Leafs will finish
fourth.
                He's reading T.S. Eliot, as usual
enjoying the images, jumping off
the train.

                He recorded his five-pin
bowling scores, with J the left-handed,
166–119, 116–145, 232–107. Life
is sweet.

                The city any time
can expect sunshine and warmth. This
is life, nor is he eager
for now
to get out of it.

Banality is all right, competition
is something like poetry, it lasts
for a second, and it means
nothing but itself.

SUMMER 1959. Oliver

They drove up to a mosquito-infested spot
this side of Bridesville for a picnic,
for the wind on the hills,
the low hill is spattered
with loose earth —

Chico rolled in wet cow manure
so he threw him into a creek twice.
He was sorry.

Below, there is, they see,
a beauty in this valley,
where the earth is largely stone.

FALL 1959. Vancouver

The history prof is much the same this year.
The political science prof is quite dull

as a hyacinth,
hidden in a far valley,
perishes upon burnt grass.

The leaves are still on the trees, most
of them green in the wind

that turns them, to look them over.
The English prof is a ludicrously pompous

poseur.
        We all perish
before the streets are too wet for sparks.

WINTER 1959. Oliver

He and Willy had a few beers
at the Oliver hotel. Then they drove
Windy Bone & the other Indian to their horses.

What note shall we pitch?
We have a song,
on the bank we share our arrows;
the loosed string tells our note.

Sally is working nights and he is working days.
They havent seen one another for a long time.
Apparently a man died in her arms last night.

No coffee or poetry for him any more.
No more buzzing words in his ear.

Willy wondered whether they would see them
leave. But Windy
wanted them to ride their horses in the crisp moon.

No, they said, thank you, Windy, but no.

SPRING 1960. Vancouver

He bought a baseball glove
and a book of poems,

he saw Warren Tallman with his
omnipresent coffee thermos.

How many times a day do you fill that up, he asked.
Enough to keep me percolatin', was the reply.

You cannot win the Nobel Prize
playing baseball. Cannot call the muse.

O flight,
bring her swiftly to our song.

Desolación
by Gabriela Mistrál.

The coffee keeps us awake.
The poems wake us up.

SUMMER 1960. Vancouver

A widening circle of world
takes him downtown for a second time today,

to the art gallery, there's Tessai
on paper, there's an old bishop

lecturing in Japanese, tough *samurai* voice
and tiny yellow head, nearly transparent,

bends this ancient pottery head over paper,
his purple robe falling exact.

Young B's knuckles feel like rough bolts,
his pants feel sticky in the middle.

Bishop was Tessai's chief student, students
come in all sizes. Now he's doing calligraphics

and young B'll get one, it'll be there
on his study wall when he's someone else

remembering a silver watch on the old man's thin left wrist,
the *Nissei* girl flattening rice paper for his quick brush,

remembering he nearly expired
each time he saw her angelic breasts.

FALL 1960. Vancouver

First month of lectures
in his fifth year of studies

in early morning sleep time
high on the second story

of someone else's house,
for the first time since he wore a hat

he pissed the bed. Had to
bundle sheets to the laundromat.

She said he has been running fast
to the toilet lately, he might have

a bladder infection. He might years later
write a poem containing

history or a bladder infection. They ride to school
on bicycles, which is fine

but damned wet on head and legs
in the Autumn West Point Grey rain.

WINTER 1960. Oliver

Night after night of liquor,
oily stuff in his clothes.

Waiting for the Greyhound bus,
they went bowling. She bowled

while he went for a mickey of rum,
then they bowled, poor things.

Five pins.

> *The hard sand breaks,*
> *and the grains of it*
> *are clear as wine.*

She dropt his bottle splash on the floor.
It was partly for the bus.

He went for another
while she bowled some more.

He always writes down his scores,
but not in poems. She had a pull

on the bottle, a push on him.

SPRING 1961. Vancouver

Exploration an easy trope,
the new so tiring, the sweet
so near;
            that is he partied with her
for twenty-four hours, it was
Corinna's 21st birthday, her swain
forty-five, English, an actor, let our hero
drive his Daimler, rev its
Rolls-Royce motor.
                  They drank at her place
till eleven, caught Rolf Harris
at the Arctic Club, heard the Mary Kaye Trio
at the Cave, dined and danced
at the Penthouse, champagne
till breakfast, champagne
for breakfast.
              Life with her
was always like this, champagne and peaches
for lunch, music and games
all day,
        till they had to rush,
to make a dinner date,
sip drinks surrounded by polished wood.

If he was going to be what he was,
he could continue this Rolls-Royce life
or something else,
                      would he continue
something else?

SUMMER 1961. Oliver

The sun is down, he stands
fully awake
        and wonders what sleep is

in this vapidity, no one
living in his home town desires

anything but the new television,
they wish to see no further

than a man on a horse, a man
with a gun, a father who after all

did know best.
        He, on the other hand,
knows nothing, he's twenty-five, he

was the only person in the house
who watched *The Human Voice* of

Cocteau last night. He's writing a novel,
he thinks, no one else does, but

he only watches the ball game, he
keeps score and announces the hitters.

He likes the word "cerebral," he
uses it while characterizing his townspeople.

FALL 1961. Vancouver

Oh clarity to come,
He played eighteen holes with Lee Mackenzie
and a guy named Mac.

Burnished-head
by burnished-head
they bent over the adequate greens
of the UBC links.

And we ask this — where truth is,
of what use is valour and is worth?

He parred two of the par-threes,
he heard his loan was coming through,

he attends no lectures after Wednesday
of the week, he is a quarter

of a century in age. Later
he will likely know what now

he never dreams of, eyes well focused
to bear that little white ball

on its dimpled way.

WINTER 1961. Vancouver

Amusing & otherwise, life goes like episodes, like an idiot
in the face of joy.

He writes an examination
on linguistics.
He records a radio broadcast
with Earle Birney.
He has a scene with one woman
& meets the other.
The other is on the phone saying "that's it"
to her other man.
On his way there he gets his first ever
traffic ticket.
Back in the car he finds it to be
empty of gasoline.
He has to push it half a block to park
uphill.
He has to walk six blocks for gasoline &
six blocks back again.
Later he drives this, his first car,
many many miles, yes
with his hand brake on. He's in love
& losing his girl, & finding
it a little cold, surrounded by Santas
& he's falling in love, & he can
hardly wait to get famous, like a comic strip
in panels.

"SPRING"* 1962. Oliver

Unable to stop the jangle in his heart,
he carries home from the small familiar post office
two fat letters from his darling today,
three in two days, oh wings,

alas he has them not, not
swift, a bird,
set of God
among the bird-flocks!

Her letters come to him in the desert
from a non-existent place, words
out of nowhere near the green sea.

She barely exists while he loses
these precious summer days away from her,
¡*que lástima!*
               and what an empty sky.

But he is home, and who is this
inside him now, hurting his body inside,
echoing the pain where wings would be?

---

* An error. Instead of Spring, we will get Summer twice.

SUMMER 1962. Oliver

I have lately been feeling good about being young.
Finished an essay for my poetics book

I'll take years writing. Three fat letters
at the post office, from my "baby," arrive

from a non-existent coast, she exists I guess
while I'm here. He's here. This young poet

country newspaper man, loses "precious days"
away from her. Meanwhile he reads

a novel by touted James Purdy. This
is what he writes: "he like other young

Americans has an ear for dialog, but pic-
ayunes away at boring days in a dull life."

Bad enough to live them without knowing.

FALL 1962. Vancouver

Inside the strangeness of living
as a young man, with.

With A, they went to see his
soppy hero, nearly jazzman, Sammy
Davis Junior, at the Queen.
Elizabeth Theatre. It was very nice
to see him at last, gratifying
to hear him do Frank Sinatra
the white guy.

        Snow. C.P.
Snow sees the continent of the rich
pull away from the continent poor.

We need, he says, to revampire
western education, supply money, send
men to poor lands, prod
their revolutions. China, 1949.

But intellectuals. They are rooted
in the so far
all right soil of the past. They do impressions
(if you want unity) of the past. This
is tradition. Not the strange.

WINTER 1962. Vancouver

Al Purdy writes and he's never met him,
pronouns sliding all over the personal,
he says profuse thank-yous for my work
to bring him here
                    for what
will be war, & I a victim, no
there's no way I'd know that yet.

He does, I do, enjoy all this
widening circle of world, letters falling
from fingers widened far from here.

I thought of a cocktail party today,
my circle of friends never in the city,
my new wife at work, all this

writing with Purdy, McFadden, O'Broin.
Here in the city he never hears a word
about poetry. If there is a muse

she must have a postal address.

SPRING 1963. Vancouver

She and he had some *hermosa* time tonight,
new frontiers in geography and extremes
in before dinner in-
terim.

More than compensates for fear and tension,
this healthy cinema for supper.

Being in love, he thinks, with a girl
you have liberty to live with all night and day,
is better than being in anything else.

SUMMER 1963. Vancouver

Am I the god?
or does this fire carve me
for its use?

The romantic poet falls back on intensity of feeling rather than striving for clarity & precision.

He lies in bed till the jangling is gone from his head, then rises and begins a poem by natural light.

He doesnt believe that man is a super creature exalting his soul over a world made of things transformed by the superior imagination.

•

A man is more interesting
than man.

Neither is true, both sound swell,
god and fire.

He loves the bush,
not the voice in the bush.

FALL 1963. Calgary

Five miles to midnight
it is better to taste of frost —
the exquisite frost —
than of wadding and of dead grass.

Trying to be suspenseful,
the lead players skulked around the city
looking guilty enough for an infant
to suspect. Wadding in the script

brought midnight no nearer,
Paris no closer, murder
no colder. No heart
beats in that dull garden.

It is better to taste of Alberta frost
than the servings of Anatole
Litvak.

WINTER 1963. Oliver

Pry apart the timid souls,
he said, driving 450 miles

of frozen roads, the Rockies
behind them now, A

weeping for the young dog
dead at the vet's, a likely

incompetent. Here the new
puppies help her, and here

family banality and snow, what
a relief, calamity beyond belief.

But tobagganing on the old
golf course, his father behind,

they set a record pace, and jumped
into somersault, into snow crash,

dad flying over him, fetched
his ear a wallop with his boot,

the other people laughing their
heads off at the top of the hill.

SPRING 1964. Calgary

Not a doer but an observer, inside
in-sane wrigglings of the night before —

strained isolate earlier today after
fourteen hours of sleep, safe away,

standing in kitchen reading Fitzgerald notes
in New Directions book, or was that also

last night, tycoon of snow, at silent
normally tasty dinner, below zero

wind outside. He shovelled snow in
white blindness, sex organs no longer

a-perk, slyly reading, a book on the bed,
a book on the kitchen table, magazine

on the couch, an artbook on the
coffee table. He goes from one to

another, an architect of the day, a maze
in Christian underworld, also silent!

of aeons ago, outside himself silent.

SUMMER 1964. MÉXICO

He saw his first rhino
in Chapultepec Park, old Aztec
forest.
        Brückner's Second Symphony
and Maximiliano's last palace,
                never quite
been in Europe, he,
                    sits on a hill of trees
and sees all Mexico City, all Carlota.

Max in Mex would die, never
go back to Trieste.

            You dwell in your father's house,
            The gold-wrought porches of Zeus,
            apart in the depth of space.

2.

            Bent old Yanquis with newspapers
sit in Cuernavaca's three squares,
                    persistent
boys with Chiclets harass the newcomers,

a lovely park surrounded by wall-spilled buganvilla
lies green, waits for afternoon rain
to clean the dust, make a green place
for a strange African animal.

FALL 1964. Calgary

University of B.C. lecturer Lionel Kearns
has been awarded, this is the only way,
a Canada Council Scholarship, a Canadian poet,
to study at London School, can get his picture,
of Oriental Studies, in the paper.

If there are connections, dont make them.
Got a letter from Lionel today, I guess
you could say he's my best friend.

He's in England now that Fall is here,
after a great mustache in Cuba, drear
visit to Trinidad, multi-racist Island,
Island, Island, Lionel
is spending all his time on Islands,
connections made by airports.

The Canada Council has just announced
it wants to keep our students at home;
our poets can go to Hell, where
no man is a connection.

WINTER 1964. Toronto

Veracruz about as far east as Winnipeg,
A took her first subway ride,
she's an oven
unlighted.

Saw Harold Town's "Enigmas," this is truly
the big city his country
is capable of. Veracruz is a kind of Marseilles
filled with brown people,
heavy birds on the roof, no snow,
and saw a collection of Op-type
        social oil statements by that famous
        Vancouver painter, what's
        his name?

Veracruz is southwest of here, Hart Crane dead,
they walked wet pavement of Bloor Street
looking at stylish,
looking at what they dont have in Alberta,
say,
a mist in the December air, a taffrail,
a song played on a beach,
a poet having a poet to dinner,
wives happily there.

SPRING 1965. Oliver

He thinks he could play
good golf if he played
all the time. He could
quit smoking, waste

no time at all.
He and Tony went round
with Mom and Dad.
It was warm, or

what they call here
in the South Okanagan
cold;

>   *leave the stark core*
of the rose
to perish on the branch.

SUMMER 1965. Oliver

She suspects an infant
starts to grow inside them,

while outside her sister calls
for a beauty in this valley.

Only in moments of cricket
or horizon does it appeal to him.

But a baby now. Holding
his sister's baby, he let her appeal

a little, to him.

FALL 1965. Calgary

He doesnt know what to do about his dog
Frank's new habit of pissing on people.

Today he tried to piss on Tony
but only got the couch.

Then while he was whacking him
his other dog Small got so scared

he emptied his bladder on the mattress.
Then Frank pissed on the floor.

And he, stumbling, kicked over their water dish.

He should forget animal order
and concentrate on his stamp album

but he's run out of hangers.

WINTER 1965. Vancouver

Despite this it'll be ghastly at the end,
but now he walks in cotton pants, denim shirt,
feels free in the Coast clime,

saw Moan Collins, old Moan, did the fucking
shopping, went and saw Mike Rice, old
painter, saw Glad-Eyes for a moment,

old Keep-a-Movin' is in California, damn
the routed vocables, others are dead, Warren
of the Introduction is out for dinner,

see him tomorrow when he's tamer, these
Coast people wearing secret names from his books,
cant see him, he's invisible in their pages.

And here he's accused of taking "another
pen of mine." But here it says black medium,
has his own teeth marks on the end. So he

drinks his li'l orange joose and vodka, you bet.

SPRING 1966. CALGARY

It's supposed to be
the beginning of spring.

Eternal concerns vex and charm
the human image, such as

Paul Newman! The left-handed
gun boy, Billy, his strivings

are dust. He, the movie viewer,
supports one George Stevens,

he says American movies, dont
deride them, they are as good

as her European films. Winter
is supposed to be gone, some

of his best friends are American
movie personalities.

SUMMER 1966. Düsseldorf

A lame duck last day in Europe
first time, six weeks in a Bug
now packaged for a ship.

                        Tomorrow
if he's lucky the DC-7 will stay up
eighteen hours, a silver crate
with Pacific on its skin over North
Atlantic, filled with busybody German
Canadians and yowling babes in hammocks,
the classical event that makes
a family of us all.

Waiting for tomorrow and Amerigo,
he blows bubbles, good Bazooka pink
he got for ten *pfennigs* in a machine
on the Krautish street. He cant read
the wrapper comics, she

hates it when he buys gum,
waits for him in that other continent
heart.

FALL 1966. Toronto

Il faut se rendre, it is moist and windy
after that sunny automobile highway from the west.

He sees Earle as always, wheeling, dealing, weighing
university offers, women, writing, a hot car,
speaking, as they say, engagements.

He has an odd feeling of discontent or unbalance,
walking around in prose. No emotion endures.

Last night he met them all at last,
Toronto bards, they had to be,
Rosy Joe and sweet bp.

In a few days he has to find a house,
domestic lout in a new town, iambic.

He gives up, gives up the thought of giving up,
prose exuded from his ears, sidewalks defiled.

He spends five dollars for four white pills
for a small dog who loves poetry and meat.

WINTER 1966. London

More and more the poets
get their pictures in the papers.

He doesnt know whether that means our world
is getting better

or falling apart. We have no home
save sickness,

a cold coming, a second
between fire and fire.

SPRING 1967. London

Snowing and melting, central
Canaday is March, time to read, he said,
the Fried North Throwup poets, Le
Pang! , Mac
Person! , James Rain
Man! , but hey, this one's pretty
good!

Time, he said, to go to the
York!, sit in on
drums! with the Nihilist Spasm
Band!
        Yor k-no good,
they said, keep slipping
into time.

        And away
to another bar where two drunken men
walk into the women's toilet.

And outside in Ontario
it is snowing out the night sky,
you should be home
standing in right field.

Poem? You can
finish it

[   ]

SUMMER 1967. London

There were literary gents around,
one of them Creeley, he is a friend
& reads a story full of noise
out of a strange little magazine,
laughing, excited. Is this Creeley?

Duncan made him stop, interrupting
time & again till Creeley argued
it's best to quit reading. To quit dream
he woke up.

     His wife A
says this is a homosexual story. This day
the humidity is gone, he can walk
to the store quickly, on Oxford Street
at noon, at noon.

FALL 1967. Montreal

The city feels world exposition
fear, and now a "wildcat"
transit strike, yes, sure,

downtown there are pretty women
hitchhiking in fur coats, long
slow traffic jams. He is

writher in residence going crazy,
a friend's kid pulling Mexican
pots off tables. Too low, fear

of a red-headed kid, he buries
in *The Ginger Man*, light reading,
an easy wing. He regrets nothing.

He thinks of the cities he likes:
San Francisco, México, Istanbul,
Tucson, London,
Vancouver. Here.

WINTER 1967. Montreal

"He is one of a thousand
non-descript
 college types.

He's an observer, not
 a doer.

He does not dwell
in his own house.

 He has left
the stark core of the rose
to perish on the branch, tough

as petals.

 The plot is an old one
with a modern day treatment,

an evening of light reading,
close enough to dry her tears."

SPRING 1968. Montreal

Curnoe and Fones and he stood in no jazz room
drilling the great Zeppelin mural into place

not place but under-apron path, Dorval
airport, passing Yankee Expo tourists

hauling suitcases full of ironed chinos,
hands stuffed with passports and green dough.

Till the Mounties came their subterranean way
and made them take it down, holes in stone,

all that beautiful Canadian work, take panel
down by panel. Someone had complained

re text, a hand-painted citation from *Freedom*,
re Muhammad Ali and Vietnam. War

Expo, no habitat under concrete. They
departed their tunnel, Cong with art

under arms, a grim angry snort from Greg,
his airship pal, a Canadian walking east,

into U.S. arrivals.

SUMMER 1968. Calgary

They drove back over the Rockies
to keep his brothers out of jail,
staying five more days till they could
enter their pleas. This late sixties dope scene
playing out its parodic end in Cow Town.

Doubling back; they had just done
their Calgary time, he'd just unpacked
his books and pens in the Okanagan, dogs
running in their parents' yard. Later
travel plans screwed by Calgary. Family?

Well, family. How odd to have brothers
growing up, going to jail. This time
they saw only a glimpse of a bear on
the Trans Canada. Forked out $75
for Marty's bail, his brothers couldnt find it all.

And he doesnt think that Alan and Heather
are overjoyed to see them back so soon.
And he's got a headache centered in
his left eye.
And they have to drive back, with brothers.

This is how families are formed,
stories are started,
youth is spent.

FALL 1968. MONTREAL

The coffee keeps them awake,
the television gets older and older.

He watched in awe plus chagrin
as the Calgary Stampeders clobbered the
Tigercats, aw darn it, in Hamilton.

In Hamilton McFadden sits all night
scrutinizing print, perfect place
for a poet. He's watching with dis-

ease as the Stampeders reach within
seven points of Ottawa. A is
a football widow. He is a Canadian.

There are [tumbleweeds, no] twelve weeks to go till
Christmas holidays, equinox is here,
it is 80 degrees Fahrenheit. In Calgary

it is freeze and snow. They'll never
live there again. He has no poet
to quote. That was "almost intercepted."

WINTER 1968. Montreal

Eternal concerns vex and charm
our artful lives, headache, stuffy
nose, sore limbs, work on
radio tapes suspended, Curnoe
is here to finish the airport mural
but the propeller motors are stolen,
no tape recorders are available,
they dont even consider the season,
when Tony arrives, headache,
stuffed sinuses, sore legs, New York
in a few days, she is in bed
coughing, the painter & the poet
and the prairie friend do last minute
shopping, while around the only moon
turn Anders and Borman and Lovell,
looking back at us, look at the big blue.

SPRING 1969. Wolfville

A short-hair kid with a Fiat sports car
drove him there, sixty miles

to the faculty club. He smiled as best he could
while a salesman English professor wanted to know

where he could publish his poems. A sociology guy
persuaded him that these apple valley kids

are getting a second-rate education. He drank
as fast as they'd let him, ate as quick as he could.

•

Then, here comes the usual sestet and sentiment:
he remembered animal order, he went home to play

crokinole with Greg Cook's children, *ah,*
squalor was cheated at last, for a bright head

flung back told him when this is over with
we get a late night bed time snack.

SUMMER 1969. Toronto

Of course the reading in the stadium fell through, but of course McClelland & Stewart paid his train fare. Of course the festival is hype, some business people and a football field, a person named Eaton and a person named Walker. Said of course Coach House and Rochdale couldnt put up a booth, might sell some books and magazines.

That big crowd
was not enlightened
not charming
nor even friendly,
not even to the musicians.

Victor says
that's Toronto at the end of the sixties.

So they got their counterfeit tickets and listened:
The Velvet Underground, Johnny Winter, Procol
Harem. Enjoying the images, jumping
off the train.

All those writers and poets
trying to forgive, trying not
to lord it over those popular celebrities,
eh, Barrie? People wearing velvet
at midsummer, even the colour
wrong.

FALL 1969. Montreal

He let her appeal, a little,
to him,

> *a curious peril, this —*
> *the gods have invented*
> *curious torture for us.*

They exhaust her, who brought
as always her novel for them,

consulting. Of their marriage
she is always ready to talk,

and he does,
             about himself, too.

and he hears her buzzing voice
describe his choice.

WINTER 1969. Montreal

"The seed planted by Kerouac
and tended by Kerouac and others
is now bearing fruit,
and although B isn't rich and famous,
hasn't sold any scripts to Hollywood,
he's doing what he wants and knows
he'll be remembered for it."

— David McFadden

Nineteen years later he's tending
to forget him already,

this Bowerbird in a fruit tree;
he dropped a seed a minute

as our winged friends tend to do,
and whoever cares, oh

axe that tree, bring that bird
to me.

SPRING 1970. Montreal

Her buzzing voice
enters the forest
where she looks so hard
to see spooks
she doesnt find myth.

*Though we wander about,
find no honey of flowers in this waste,
is our task the less sweet?*

The lady talks about the
data of her life,
stepping off the boat, facing
the real forest.

Through the forest the keen eye
can see the ground cleared
for the U of T.

SUMMER 1970. Montreal

The same sorry rut
not between
          peaches filled with honey
but before the day's television

though he ground out four and a half pages
on jazz and the short poem.

You dwell in your father's house —

He filled out a form for *Who's Who*,
his shortest fiction so far,

though he smoked a cigar with a plastic tip
and got the titles of his volumes correct,

bibliographer.

FALL 1970. Montreal

*Your fellow wretches
will crowd to the entrance —
be first at the gate.*

They went over to
their semi-friends', they saw
their recent baby, as ugly
as most.

        She suspects
an infant crowds them or will.
Their semi-friend has fancied
up his house;

he must owe someone
thousands of dollars.

WINTER 1970. Montreal

She does not dwell in her father's house.
She "received" news of his death
last night. First at the gate

then in her heart,
broken and deep
hurt behind her Christmas tree.

Her sister watching his badly behaved body
disappear, husband broke, brothers
adamant, an independent clause
at her wits' end, history in frozen
Island ground.

Their friend's letter pops through the slot.
He wonders what will ruin their Yule
this year. Can she, can she
grin when he gets here? Her own house?

SPRING 1971. Oliver

Horsing around like a man, he grew excited
driving into the Valley, Valley folk
love capital Vees, Tenney in the car,
out of the car, they can walk
without coats, a little ice on the lakes.

Home was never sickness as other places
were, yesterday they all looked
at his grade two house in Greenwood, fresh
bushes behind it. Here he meets his
sister-in-law and niece, one of whom

promptly and silently pees in his lap.
His dad went curling and he observed,
and then placed Tenney on the midnight bus.
It is plainly ordinary in his mountain
fastness, he walked to his brother's place

giving thought to buying a pre-fab house.

SUMMER 1971. Vancouver

A's in the kitchen,
she's an oven,
making baby cake.

This is a commune
he's out of,
at Simon Fraser University
looking for a job.

Fred and Pauline are here
making old connections.

rain,   He gave a paper to the profs,
              a class to the students,
              a straight line to poor sick ears.

no   He wants to bring up this body in
             Vancouver,
ball   but does he need a job in that ill place?

practice   He stokes the stove,
              he averts the gaze,
              he takes his turn
              on cooking days.

FALL 1971. Vancouver

Keep slipping into time, tomorrow
the baby's due, they have at
last a first
name, Thea, because all the dreams
say it's a girl, she's an it
self.
      Today his new book arrived, its name
is Touch, of course,
              and Tenney said
looks like you've got the job, everything
happens at once, and that isnt the
½ of it.
      D brought some hash
and a knitted shawl for the bairn,
why knot?
      Dont, said D, get
excited, wrap yourself in this
smoke.
      They worked on his
manuscript, of course, bring a book
into the world,
          a job can wait
till all this is begun.

WINTER 1971. VANCOUVER

Before he left Lawrence this time he was rooting around in the cellar, looking for a brick or a two-by-four to go with his baby, and he saw a vertical cubbyhole where he used to keep his collection of broken baseball bats. It came to his mind that he might remember stashing something there when he was a kid. He dipped his arm through the spiderwebs and came up with his October 1947 *Sunbathing for Health* magazine. He remembered every archer and every beach ball nude, all the grey photos he had looked at so often, their air-brushed genitals. Inside the magazine was his 1946–1947 certificate that proved he was a junior Maple Leafs fan. His father had been a Canadiens fan. His father knew it said affiliated, but he had a good laugh when his son read aloud: officially afflicted with the Toronto Maple Leafs. Slipping *out* of time, too.

SPRING 1972. Vancouver

He's had Brückner's
third symphony out of the jacket
for days, but never
gets the chance to play it.

Weed, moss-weed,
root tangled in sand,
puddles at shortstop
make his footing something

other than baseball. He and
his mother took Gumpy
for a long walk in the buggy.

He hardly saw his mother and daughter,
but rather Honus Wagner at short,
a devout music of stumpy flesh.

SUMMER 1972. Vancouver

He begins to despair of seeing
serious critics in his life
time for his life's
work.
        The reviewers chase after
a major writer among old hacks
back east, or coo excitedly
after a personality.
                Oh, depend on it,
he writes of serious, maybe eternal
concerns that vex and charm
the human mind, but no commentator
notices.
        They cluck over the subject
of the apparent state of his emotions.

One might as well despair
or pose for front porch snapshots
with the Greeks across the street.

If it looks as if nothing will develop,
get together again, take another,
that's the Greek way. Regret nothing.

FALL 1972. Vancouver

He asked Joseph Brodsky
what's the difference between the Leningrad poets
and the Moscow poets.

                      The baby had
fallen down the stairs her first time,
old tears round her eyes.

                      They are
more sophisticated, the Leningrad poets,
in the good sense, he replied.

                      The poet
Lionel Kearns bent over his plate, finished
his pie while his friend was half way
through his salad.

                      The woman
from the Russian Department surrounds
the Leningrad poet with deans and
chairpersons.

                      Separated by a table,
the Vancouver poets bent their heads
and ate, some more politely than others.

WINTER 1972. Vancouver

The bills unpaid, un-
payable, the cheques written
cannot be mailed, the bank
is empty, the poor little tree
is atop a stereo speaker,
the new dishwasher gleams.

Was Whitman right? Should he
dance? He has a pain
behind his left eye, they
have no sickness save home
but a child separated from a tree
by a chair. They

save her from pulling it over
on herself, she who
never sits anyway. Was
Duncan right? He makes a poem
ending with a word called Pindar.

SPRING 1973. Burnaby

"He has consistently amazed Canadians with his poetic ineptitude and public relations ability.

"I felt sad that a grown man could stand up there and make such an ass of himself, displaying his lack of intellect and invisible technique.

"His poems are for the most part strung-out, contorted, awkward, and generally fucked-up.

"B and his crew are body stealers, scrounging on the scraps and remains of their predecessors, milking what they can from their betters.

"I have heard incredible visions and perceptions of the visible and invisible world from half-crazed anarchist loggers.

"There is a need for such conversation between the community of poets."

— B.T. Brett

SUMMER 1973. Vancouver

Why learn to speak at all?
If only to enter a stupid dispute
with a crazed poet in a redneck magazine?

Why not quietly produce a new book
and call him your old pal,
make up a life together?

Life with him was always
like that, a barrel of sobs, a
red face and a red face, a

squirrel on a bird-feeder, a
dodging of libel, hey, Miltie,
I loved your poem about Lycidas,

I thought that was a good drug,
keeps you forgetting the great war
and the great failure at war.

Soon a painter will show up,
come round, drop over, fall by,
make a brush with greatness,

put an end to speech.

FALL 1973. Vancouver

He worked diligently along the beach,
raking piles of human eyeballs.

He took the first copy
of Warren's little booklet over today,
his first separate publication.

Warren went to another room
for a hanky. "Honk!"
What's that? asked the child.

She's nearly two. That's
my house, she said earlier.
"That's, ah, wonderful," said Warren.

Life with her
              was always like this.

WINTER 1973. Vancouver

No drinks, no polished wood,
and no one will ever know

whether the picture he saw clearly
as in a mirror included a child

or only old age. She came home hot
from the daycare, had no real supper,

she asked to go to bed at six. She
had a little nosebleed at the party

and now looked funny round the eyes.
All day at the party the big kid Jordan

knocked her off things. Why learn to speak
and then have only ill health to say?

He looked into the future, and all he saw
was gold, frankincense, myrrh, soil.

SPRING 1974. Vancouver

Brian won the first game of snooker
and he came second.

*Will you fling your spear-head
on the shore?*

Dwight won the second game
and he tied for second.

I break a staff.

Brian won the third game
and he tied for second.

I break the tough branch.

Then they played a bunch of poker pool
and when it was over Dwight came first
and he came second.

*I know no light in the woods.
I have lost pace with the wind.*

SUMMER 1974. Vancouver

Daphne called, the Bau-Xi Gallery
is on fire, the whole block
is smoke & red light.

The kid isnt three, someone
has to watch her while her mother
takes a warm bath for her shrink.

We have to save the paintings —
Boy! fifty miles an hour down Forty-First,
leave the kid with Grandma

then fifty miles an hour the opposite direction,
there, thigh-deep in freezing water,
hauling out paintings by Roy and others

> *in that clear place*
> *where the women dip*
> *their water-jars,*

no time to reflect on the death of art.
When he brings hours later a painting home,
he has to hang it in his room

away from the anger, go get the kid,
figure out dinner.

FALL 1974. Vancouver

It is 80 degrees Fahrenheit. In
Vancouver
the Granville Grange Zephyrs beat
the Flying Dildos 24–19. Post-season
baseball as lovely as having

a daughter nearly three. They had together
the morn, the game, Queen Elizabeth
Park, a visit to Dwight's place,
five new kittens. Be careful, he said

like an idiot in the face of joy.
He and Dwight proofread the last pages
of an anthology, what a Sunday, warm
as a new feline belly. He watched

in awe as well as chagrin. What
a stupid dad, be really careful, he
cautioned. Cautious. A caution. A cat
might get you, a line drive

might break your cheekbone ten years
from now. Look out. Dwight
is a poet he once shamelessly quoted,
no, stole from.

WINTER 1974. Vancouver

          This is tradition,
not the strange.
          She makes good use
of the NY *Times* cook book he got
as introduction to that book club. He's
getting a belly

          full. "B
reveals that it's easier to write
poems about nothing than it is to write
short stories about nothing."

Ian Dunn died on the highway
ten years ago, his funeral last night
occurred in a cave. When he was
carried in I saw his head bobbing.
Etc.

          Little Gumpy,
    with her small stem glass,
    has become something of an expert
    wine fancier,

a short story becoming more familiar
with time.

SPRING 1975. Vancouver

Her buzzing voice,
almost, this afternoon,
talks about writing,

Peggy, he didnt say
what you say he said,
he didnt have it in his head,

but he is happy to see you
listen. To get some
of the attention.

We forgot — for a moment
tree-resin, tree-bark,
sweat of torn branch
were sweet to the taste.

SUMMER 1975. Vancouver

The day he went two for three
his friend Tenney tried to sell
a three-wheeled motorcycle, closed in,
a steering wheel for steering,

a bad idea, said Tenney, asking
$250, if you're heading for a
collision, the other driver
doesnt know your intention.

And he was put out, nervous now,
he was trying to sell a motorcycle too,
made two errors at short,
laid down a perfect bunt,

making up a life together.

FALL 1975. Vancouver

Not a deer but an observer, wangled
a free pass to the novelist show at UBC,

bearer of a .298 batting average, sat down
for free lunch. Six hundred people and he

is the last to get his roast beef, piled
other people's roast potatoes on his plate.

The mid-seventies fiction life, playing ball
on teams with silly names, blowing the relay,

routing the vocables, charms him while
he seems to sleep. Peggy A comes over again,

says she hopes she's pregnant, kid wont
play ball in 2015 A.D. Robert K looks

good, maybe grey. Audrey T managing
humour. There's a blonde trash novelist

tries to stay sexy in boutique clothes,
says she's an awetist.
                        He gets roast beef

at gigs like this, wrote a novel once,
gave it a serious name.

WINTER 1975. Vancouver

All these visits when the earth seems
to tilt away,
              now, for instance, in Cuba,
we are all in green or brown fatigues
and the sun is down, we
simply lie on the ground, young
men and women, to sleep.

Strength.
To endure.

But in the small university classroom
a middle-aged female professor
and a middle-aged male professor
urge their sociology on us,
standing up clean, big clean eyeglasses.
Explaining the young revolutionaries.

Buy.
That makes him mad.

He'd rather lose something
and slowly come to realize
it's gone.

SPRING 1976. VANCOUVER

She's watching *The Red Shoes*,
getting educated on PBS, while he

remembers his boring childhood, no
Winnie the Pooh, no Alice

in Wonderland. But A,
who remembers everything, says

this movie gets ghastly at the end,
she did read him Winnie and Alice, that

was their honeymoon, he says
I'll take her out for an hour

before the hockey game, his boring
adulthood, except for this, this

having a future, getting educated,
stepping off the boat, facing the real

forest or the Washington Capitals.

SUMMER 1976. Vancouver

How does he know it'll be ghastly
at the end? At the front door
of their cottage he saw the door knob
explode, then was inside
a roaring. His body figured out
he was being shot at from behind.
A never before experienced thing
in the whole right side of his body,
he had no time to get inside, now
the strangeness of dying, what form,
no help, he tried to call for help
but his voice is a whisper. Awake
in bed he whispers for help but A
in the next room cannot hear him,
he cannot move to see. He is awake
and dying, they did not require of him
that he keep a day free.

FALL 1976. Vancouver

Island, Island, I wish I were no man.
In the basement, doing laundry,
in the kitchen, doing supper,
in the lineup, buying canned goods,
four-year-old at the table.

2:45, Mom leaves for dinner groceries
again; 7:30, others go for hamburgers
again; 12:45 a.m., Mom comes home
again, cant walk straight.

                        One day
Mom tried to cook supper, couldnt make the spaghetti sauce
work. What's wrong, Mom, says
four-year-old at the table with crayons;
Mom says to Dad, very loud, "If your fucking
friend tries to give us another of these,
he can shove it up his ass." Four-year-old
looks downward.

                        Does she think
this is normal in a kitchen? Does she know
Mom wishes she were cooking elsewhere?

He wishes he was at most an isthmus,
a continental compromise.

WINTER 1976. Vancouver

Telling the truth under the raindrops
on a walkie-talkie,
                dream of his
childhood, he knew as unattainable.

           He was familiar
with unattainable then, now
                      he has
a daughter who claims it'll snow
for Christmas.

            He's giving her
a magic talking machine, after all,
how to live in this world
where they get what they want.

        His best ever Christmas day was
1971, his daughter was two months old.

        His worst year ever
was this one.

                He's talking to himself
again, he's walking in circles.

SPRING 1977. Vancouver

He and Curnoe sat in the new jazz room
filled with the Art Ensemble of Chicago.

They didnt care how long it was, this
wonderful music in their whole systems.

Overjoyed, overjoyed, his living friend
here on the coast, these wonderful black men

before them, unbelievable instruments of sweet
torture scattered on the floor by their feat,

scary as an outdoor elevator, Greg sitting
behind his moustache, what snug harbour,

what skyway, what trumpet to those
angelic Illinois lips. You go out, you climb up,

and love is louder than you had imagined,
favors ricochet from the walls, Curnoe

is wearing stripes and they vibrate, the streets
may be filled with smoke, sirens burn down,

music whispers to the node in the centre of his brain,
speech will have to wait.

SUMMER 1977. Vancouver

His mother and his auntie
gone to Ketchikan
with Captain
Van-
couver.

New frontiers in someone's geography,

but gee,
his other half is loud
reciting all his wrongs
in fifteen years,
                        exploration
an easy trope, a tropic
trick,
      they have disagreed
about coffee again.

                    She never, she says,
attacked him with scissors or knife,
not in her life
this wife.

FALL 1977. Vancouver

David Robinson was over last night
with blue line of his book,
with cover mock-up, with
long eye lashes, deep brown eyes.

The coffee keeps them awake.
The poems burn them up.

It certainly looks good, but it looks
as if it wont be made in time
for his October reading tour, not in time
to go to Europe with it in his hand.

This long disease my life
is much the same this year.

Romantic, at last, he may never see
that book, but if the plane crashes
nobody'll ever read these words either.
Oh how I love it!

WINTER 1977. Vancouver

If there are no connections, dont make them.
Supervise the little kids, rooms familiar to all,

the great cement complex, sore throat, a care.
The first room is a giant pinball machine,

kids spread around its edge at controls.
He made some beautiful shots, right into

the hole at top. Bells ring. Get bored. Move
room to room, decide which to skip. The kids

come filing, male adults too, dads, wont
look at him, he's accused of abandoning his bunch.

But they're in the pool, T's there. He has to
look downward through windows, she's getting in.

Her rapid dog-paddle is her secret, I'm glad
she's got one, she puts down head, lifts bum

and rises from the chop where she was all the time
going. Her mother is signed up for an abortion,

not many days now. What's in all those cement rooms?

SPRING 1978. Vancouver

Feeling fairly good about being
middle-aged.

When he went away in January Dennis Wheeler died, and when he went away in March Russell Fitzgerald died. Both deaths were expected, but both were cruel to us all and especially to them. He thinks death is worse for the dying than for the survivors, though people act as if the opposite were true. Anyway it is almost that he's loath to go away again to return to the fact of another friend's death, though the one he fears most is his own during these plane trips.

"What stands out is the impossibility of resistance one feels in reading these poems, however unpalatable their content."
— Bruce Whiteman

SUMMER 1978. Vancouver

Yesterday they had lunch with the poet.
This was just before his reading.

T has four more days of Grade One.
He has lately been feeling bad about getting old.

If they were an art gallery
they'd be on fire.

He and the poet were friendly as always.
He likes him save for one thing.

He is glad too that T is still so young.
Looking ahead with misgiving. Tender wings.

Any symphony by Brückner, played loud enough
will please you if you're just starting middle age.

If he just didnt have this terrific desire
to be taken seriously. But I sympathize too.

At lunch he didnt have time to eat everything.
There was hardly anyone at his reading.

FALL 1978. Vancouver

At a tryout camp for football team
we late arrivals were handed, we who were
not expected to make it were handed
not football uniforms but priest robes,
dressing gowns, sharp white shins.

There were literary gents around, the coach
told him to stick his body into the rush,
frightened, a hard back-hand clout
to his windpipe. He sends no
string of pearls.

                  The regulars without
shoulderpads, with large numbers, black
red & white, dark, huge arms.
There would be no padding
in his robe, little vocation, he was late
dressing
         as when he got fired up north,
from the survey gang. He said you did this
last year, B, failure.

He ran up the stairs, his shoes
in his left hand.

WINTER 1978. Kaleden

He washed and dried her hair and now
she looks gorgeous,

a seven year old daughter,
Okanagan light through blonde;

she got off the Greyhound,
                        a suitcase in her hand,
                        her back straight,
                        pure food in her stomach,
                        no buzz in her voice.

The Dutch in front of them
were thankful to have seen
            mountains full of snow,
            a road black tires make
            every minute of the way.

Here over this dark lake
the dainty dogs scamper indoors,

the little girl waits
till they bound into her lap.

SPRING 1979. Vancouver

She allowed him as promised
to take her to the small perfect
French restaurant.

After they got home she
pursued her lad
                on the phone,

a sound in the dark air of this cave
when the flame is low & tidy,

and now what is it that has come to pass?
for fire has shaken my hand,
my strivings are dust.

                      He lay in bed
unable to stop
                the jangle
in his brain.

                    Unable to read
the menu in the flickering light.

SUMMER 1979. Vancouver

He went to the Cecil after work
    to drink a dream, drop a poem —

dreamt they promoted him to full
    professor, oh no, an academic fancy

only, said Jack, furniture in the room,
    like anything else, said this shortly

before he died, a linguist shut up
    lying under raindrops, the count

was three and oh, and everyone knew
    he was coming in with his fastball.

Fourteen years ago, inconsolable memories,
    that's what we have, in the Cecil

they quote Jack and denigrate the Giants,
    truly reflexive and intelligently social.

They dream beer dreams, and drink rue,
    they make pencil notations in the street.

FALL 1979. Vancouver

Kroetsch, his beard still
a little black, grinned
while looking into
a copy of *What the Crow
Said* in his left hand.

The widening circle of world
can be traced by feathers
avoiding extra innings, away games
and twin bills.

                If it's Friday
I can work for myself, he said,
having heard everything the bird
had to say, calmly putting foot
after foot, pacing out a radius

thus

getting away from the still
centre.

WINTER 1979. Vancouver

M got him up this morn
arriving with revised thesis

he must turn in this afternoon,
a circle, the end of a straight line.

He is M's advisor, fellow student,
would collaborate on a novel,

fellow actor, college
journalist, criss-cross, guest lecturer,

universities across the country, growing
older, invitee, on the island.

Throw them into a common grave,
celebrate a post-graduate degree,

open wide the yawking mouths,
pry apart the timid souls.

SPRING 1980. Vancouver

"Self-consciously clever
and indulgently obscure,

here is a charmingly irreverent
intellect confused as to how

seriously it should take
life. The arrogantly arid humour

is redeeming; the poet's
inability to get a third erection

is not." He regrets nothing.

Among his favourite cities are
Amsterdam, Sydney, Halifax, here.

SUMMER 1980. Vancouver

A notes that he finds
B in his amused terror
my spiritual kin.

It is with fond pleasure
and little of the old bafflement
I follow him to the stretcher,
to the grave, to the earth
a crawling hole. Ha. Ho.

This is not the strange now,
I mean, if meaning is more
than a hoe in the dirt, a ha,
not the strange, and not the
family trade. Oh finally

shoes will be useless save for
feet pointing upward, his best
walking shoes, shining

in the dark. Classical re
duction, makes a family of us all,
even his happy daughter.

FALL 1980. Vancouver

Later, they read his bunt,
so he bunted hard
past the charging
pitcher and first, and
the vacating second

for a hit and an RBI.
And under and under,
the wind booms:
it whistles, it thunders,
it growls — it presses the grass

and he binged a triple
off the crossbar
of the goalposts in center field.

What fun the last day of summer
to play ball with his friends,
Thane, Billy, Jim, James,
Laura and Bob.

If he can pray
he'll speak their names.

WINTER 1980. Courtenay

On the deck of the ferry
his daughter stood and then a large
helicopter flew over her, playing
Christmas music, fire
like words bursting from tree tops.

Captain, my captain, he skated
with the children, till he essayed
a crossover step, fell on his chin,
lost consciousness, the classical
relation that makes a family of us all.

On the deck nearing Nanaimo
stood Paul with Trudy pregnant,
a bit dizzy, non-smokers
and friends, his daughter

as far as possible from the poor old woman
having a heart attack in the sea-going
painted women's head. On the slip
the ambulance flashes, as he lies on the ice
his personal stars give way, rotor blades
confuse time, and they are there at last,
he is sitting now, hoping
no one skates over his glasses.

SPRING 1981. MONTREAL

He from one side,
I from the other,
converged on the same slender vase,

the best piece of glass
in the narrow shop.

There was also
a beautiful woman from Sweden.

Later he gave me his first edition
Williams, good Lord —

I send no string of pearls,
no bracelet — accept this

taken poem
to be our own.

SUMMER 1981. Vancouver

~~There, over that dark sea~~
~~the dainty *doge* has scampered indoors.~~

Love the world and stay inside it
a gently eccentric and not uninteresting personality,

the kinky cranky observer who is happy merely,
more gnarly and complex than he is sometimes

willing to let on, a man on a horse,
a man with a gun. A combination of humour

plus sense embodies the mute anger and
the ill foe surrender of a man speaking.

FALL 1981. Vancouver

Seeing that he's reading books by B's,
he can sample
Samuel Beckett, gorge on
Jorge Luis Borges, nibble
Nicole Brossard.

>   *Burnished-head*
>   *By burnished-head,*
>   *Pierides sought the bride:*
>   *They touched the flute-stops*
>   *And the lyre-strings for the dance,*

while he turns over
Adolfo Bioy Casares, adjusts to
Djuna Barnes, he smiles as best he can
while an English Professor lectures on John Bunyan.

Now that he's going through the B's,
he can take
Bryher to his bed,
he can seek a bride in Emily
Brontë, that burnished head.
                        The alphabet
settles by a low river, dark around light tents,

where the dance begins, his favourite partner is
Charlotte, and he may never have another,

oh Adam long gone, oh Clarity to come.

WINTER 1981. Venice

Here beside this dark sea
the dainty *Doge* has scrambled indoors.

How lucky they were yesterday
to see snow in St Mark's square,

how lucky today to look out their window
on people in hip waders
carrying widows across the riva.

At five-thirty in the morning
he woke to hear Italian shouted below,

from mature throats. Yesterday in the Basilica
the children's choir faltered
when the parents' applause
greeted the Cardinal's entrance from off-stage.

Later outside, the liberated boys and girls
were learning to make snowballs.

This, he told his daughter,
is what happens when you marry the sea.

SPRING 1982. México

Today he said to himself
how can you be said to be enjoying yourself
when you are in endless pain?

He hobbled from gallery to gallery.
His backbone broken like an Aztec pot
if you need a colourful local metaphor.

At Galería Pecanins the Cuevas exhibition
was closed, at the Gallery of Modern Art
Riopelle, Guston & Cartier-Bresson
cerrado.

      He enjoys this widening circle
of world, his back is shattered, the smog
chases him into Vips for lunch, the best
guacamole this side of Portland, Oregon.

He is enjoying himself, he loves travel,
he is very happy to be alone, he
is glad he can still stand in the street.

SUMMER 1982. Vancouver

This is family tradition,
not the strange.
                He went
to the shopping centre, wanting
to buy himself something, came home
with new sneakers for his daughter.

She came home from school,
ten years old, started
to write a book, ah God,
wrote from 3:30 till 10:00 p.m.,
twenty minutes for piano, wrote
while she ate her late supper,

never showed what the book would be.
Crippled Feo, the lovely cat
has one front paw and her face
in the hidden swallow's nest,
suddenly healthy sneak.

                        She,
the girl, may and may not
wear the shoes tomorrow, her father
too busy to write for a decade,
too plain for reward.

FALL 1982. Vancouver

He does not dwell
in his own house, cannot
clean his daughter's room.
                      Will she
                      frown at
                      a stranger,
                      ride her bike,
                      her mind
                      countries afar?

Electricians in every room, grinding
at something, drywallers yesterday, plumbers
tomorrow,
            his word processor
in a protective box for eight days
already.

        He will never be free,
a house is not a home but a house.
A life will never be lived.

                      His daughter
will inherit, owing a million dollars.

He breaks no staff.
He breaks no tough branch.

He knows no light
in the woods.

WINTER 1982. Vancouver

Home was never sickness but now
he has no home save in dreams,

in which a very pretty woman shows
pictures of bp Nichol who was her

husband, comic-strip maker in which
he the dreamer makes words

play, 1979, tansy in all the pages,
iambs in morpho-land, the name

the [something] *Muse*. He dreams
more panels, sick for home, in which

an old friend who does not remember
tells of a discussion concerning

whether he is there.

SPRING 1983. Vancouver

Last night in Camrose an elevated sign
by the highway into town
bore Rudy Wiebe's name and his
in lights.

        They never did that for him in L.A.!

Does the fire carve him for its use?
He flew back here today with the Detroit Red Wings,
traded words with Danny Gare and Ivan Boldirev.

*So you have swept me back,
I who could have walked with the live souls
above the earth.*

Over Vancouver a little girl in prairie clothes
said, "Mummy, look at the big green!"

SUMMER 1983. Vancouver

He marked one paper
this morning, wrote desultory letters,
typed two chapters of
Craft Slices,

you will come,
you will answer our taut hearts,

had lunch at Mr Roberts,
cleaned up garbage pails,
put away his fragrant laundry,
drove the car through the safety test,

bodies are falling from the sky,
bombs know no one,

visited Celia's remainder store,
looking forward to sitting down
in front of the Expos
game.

FALL 1983. Oliver

Home town is the still
centre he's been getting away from
all these widening circles, these

men, John the director and
Doug the camera man and somebody
younger the sound man.

Roy the friend the consultant
and Pearl the mom. A simple
little movie, the orchard, the

ball park, the dried mud, the
late slanting sunlight, the nouns
a little place is made of. A kid

never did come back to be filmed,
just this middle-aged man, all
excited, as if *he* were the kid,

as if he had brought those
tender stinking wings
to earth.

WINTER 1983. Vancouver

It's like pants that feel sticky in the middle,
this mulligan stew. You dont care

how long it is, not so hard to get into
as you'd expected, you just like being

inside it. Autographs on a cup beside you,
smoke in your whole system, the first

blood clot in your leg, ten years later where
you're outside it. Not quite half way through

if it's a book, a long way past the middle
if it's a life. Float on a joke

and go under again, whoever made this, him
and whose army? You'd like to join. But

he's in another country and another before that
and he doesnt give a shit about you. You're

neither going to make a high water mark,
you come back to this from time to time,

in your pants too long, could at least
have stayed out of the chowder.

SPRING 1984. Toronto/Vancouver

In the fireplace room at Ithaca
where there was church there was

Curious, friends to see in Ontario,
fuel to pump into wings,

metric measure to remember. Sarah
insisted on spelling her name Saraht

because she loves T as her father
adores H, a letter or ladder

to a Higher place. Fire from
these wings? Hope keeping us aloft,

an H in the heart, he says smugly,
a daughter to fate, his holding

a chocolate T last Chrismas, all these
private visits he loves and readers

stand or dont. The craft, to be plain,
looks new, not many riders in it, flying

from snow to know, he cannot kneel
but he adores you, daughters, he wings

on by your inquisitive smiles.

SUMMER 1984. Vancouver

There are pieces in the paper,
papers on the street, where

is Kerrisdale? There is lively wit in this
book, without wasting an ounce of

fuel, fully conscious of mortality,
what happened to that smile

that was on your floor an hour ago?
Mud and metaphor, he never would have

said it so smugly, but he thanks
the man, why not? True, she caught

his breath with her fingers; what is
breath? Who lives here? Not the noisy

dog next door late at night. There's
something red under the snow, a

wise woman leaves it there; if she's a poet
she's dead like the rest of them.

Thanks, he says, a long way
under his breath, thanks for the meal.

FALL 1984. Vancouver

Riding away into the east,
she denies *comedie* to them,
the shrivelled seeds

are split on the path —
the grass bends with dust.
He didnt have it in his head

to hold him back,
but he held back,
he sat his horse

and watched her ride away.
She is riding to remain
single, to remain a legend
beginning to fade.

WINTER 1984. Vancouver

Tender stinking wings —
on the phone a voice says
your poem wins a bunch
of money.

The art gallery's on fire —
at your desk the essay
lies finished, nine thousand words,
seamless, cruel and long.

Floating over the Alps —
you have three chapters
ready for the fancy
hand-printed signature, congratulate
yourself.

Arrogantly arid humour —
your book has one page to go,
they cant say
you dont use your gift of time.

Last minute shopping —
the world is getting tired of Christmas
almost as fast
as the people who live there.

SPRING 1985. Rome

One flower in the garden of his little hotel,
really a new kitten, he dreamt, skinny

as the woman writing in Italian
of Kroetsch, white it was, with brown splotches,

a flower beaten by rain, unnamed
by this lorn Canadian. Dreamt also

of his orange mother in the verandah bedroom,
young, rising from bed. Toronto birds

would love this March ground, never
find a road here. His cat would

pounce on them, a child sprung
into the world, no foes around.

He said, oh, are you in here? She
smiled on her student horsing about

like a man.

SUMMER 1985. BERLIN

If he can pray
he'll pray for them,

wife and daughter
in skies of slaughter

come to meet him in Germany
while he is in Suisse.

Bodies are falling from the sky,
bombs know no one's God.

If he can pray
he'll pray third for me,

floating over Alps
in a USAmerican jet.

FALL 1985. Vancouver

Write about the book you
liked or hated reading this summer
he asked them. Boy, are they
dumb! His boring old age
stares him in the face.

Rout the damned vocables, the phone
is Michael O, he's glad
he's going to Rome, he told them
get Mike. He thinks despite this
it'll be ghastly at the end.

Give wing to the deformities,
in Europe he had wide open
frontiers of time, he could read
and write and walk in the world
on sidewalks near sausages.

Goat-foot, not old yet, lonely
for a daughter gone in another
family's car to Cultus Lake, wearing
her new red shoes.

WINTER 1985. Vancouver

Doubling back.
Dropping his crisp red copy of *Zazie
dans le Métro* face open
in a car-wash puddle.

Dont want any rhythm
to settle into,
like to hear lines of words that step and stop.

Absolutely
not.

But he lifts the book and there
's a five-year-old inter-
view, he said
            In Lyric You Look And Say.
            In Later Long Poems
                      You Listen And Write.

You Be and Ell.

A and T are in the kitchen making
Christmas cake, lots of yelling
going on.

And on.

SPRING 1986. Vancouver

First he ate some
Barthes for lunch.

Then he decided numbers
might follow letters.

He ate some Heath
cinema for dinner.

Well over twenty
years of age. Just like that.

He may have done
a number, then left

the remainder for
someone else, perhaps

half-crazed
anarchist loggers.

SUMMER 1986. Vancouver

People seem not to follow
        the connections he will make.

Playing between raindrops
        he took a skipper on the chin.

Looking for a brick or a two-by-four
        or a dress he can be Helena
in.

    His wife really liked her,
        as who doesnt? Roger Clemens

trying to go thirteen and nothing
        understands nothing.

There are no connections, one makes
        the things that are not connections.

He enjoys doing anything
        to get a rally going, a squeeze play,

a dream in the middle of summer,
        good food but too much of it.

FALL 1986. Vancouver

Classical re-
lation makes a family of us all.

He returned from the field of play
to see after a daughter
and nine nieces, a first
nephew, named as is the fashion
Kevin. And two parents.

    And then two Albanian
communists from North
Vancouver.

He baited them, accused them,
called them idealists, conservatives,
the nineteenth century.
                           Their world
is always changing, they
believe in immutable theory,

have no children. His brother
has no politics.

          Kevin and Karl
and he in his baseball duds,
a Sunday like any other.

WINTER 1986. Vancouver

Family banality and the phone, what
relief, calamity beyond belief.

They put up
the tree

with it
's normality

for she
is there to see.

                              He proposed
                              and put up
                              or shut up
                              alternately.

He has never made much
of his feelings. He
wouldnt know how
to answer the question,
never win the prize.

The tree glistens/blisters in their eyes.

SPRING 1987. Vancouver

In shirtsleeves at last and
      standing in right field late
in practice he said it is
      this day that makes you glad
you didnt kill yourself
      in December.

The poet Brian Fawcett bent over
      the plate, finished his thought
with an awkward swing, uttered
      a nasty disappointed word
the man in right field
      handled with ease.

SUMMER 1987. Vancouver

"The tall vengeance-seeker
is a red-haired woman."

FALL 1987. WHISTLER

Talking to himself again, walking
in circles someone else designed,

they limp, he says, we
have children. See what they are

trying to resemble, while he
breaks into tears in the shower,

clock towers and painted roofs,
crooked roads wide enough for

North American fire trucks. He
imagined his daughter in a coffin,

couldnt get her out of his mind.
Here he had a yup-burger

at a bar called La Cittá, wealthy
young under umbrellas, looking

beautiful. His mind's pictures,
dont deride them, escape

the voice riding him while his tears
flowed down with the rest.

How did he drive the highway to death,
the wipers still in bright sun?

WINTER 1987. Toronto

Making a life together while
some of them are dying, some,
drifting, a Harry William Bowering
nabbed for assaulting a woman.

Gwen is dead, Stan is bereaved,
just got to know her, looked for-
ward, another island gone, bp
is over, eating a plate of cookies.

Earle had a stroke, memory slides
and it's gone. I'm leaving, he says,
on a jet plane, but Paul is over
for chicken and a hockey game on TV.

Frank is alive, but he's leaving soon,
out of town. David introduced him to
his girl, a woman from memory,
surrounded by students of some sort.

There are pieces in the paper.
There are papers in the hall.

SPRING 1988. Vancouver

Enjoying the images, jumping off the train.

He and his father are in a Niagara Peninsula
man's orchard, famous white-hair
Ontarian, right now being interviewed
on TV, something important.
                                          He breaks
the tough branch.
                      The trees are short
and filled with enormous ripe peaches
the owner is picking. His father
is after something else, he has permission
providing he leaves the peaches alone.

American movies, dont deride them.

The peaches, says his father,
are like drinking honey.

                        On the stage
Daphne dances, earlier, earlier, her shirt
rolled at her waist, her very small breasts
bare.

        His father not, then, there.

SUMMER (WINTER) 1988. CANBERRA

He loves them, he loves
being with them, his dear Aussies,
an A in the heart. They care
for each other, they fly from
know to yes.

        A long way from home
at the end. It happened that way. A
peacock in the snow would be fine,
a plane crumpled in a forest. Exploded words
catching fire, classical relation
ship in your poem, maybe.

          A curious peril,
the gods have in mind, Küsnacht
will look prosperous and lonely, a
woman walking with him will resemble
a ghost.

    But here in Canberra it is
midwinter already. They eat outdoors at long tables.
The movie gets ghastly at the end
but it isnt
the end.

Printed and bound
in Boucherville, Quebec, Canada by
MARC VEILLEUX IMPRIMEUR INC.
in March, 2000